Sax After Midnight
Moonglow...

Wise Publications
London/New York/Paris/Sydney/Copenhagen/Madrid

Published by
Wise Publications
14-15 Berners Street, London
W1T 3LJ, UK.

Exclusive distributors:
Music Sales Limited
Distribution Centre, Newmarket Road,
Bury St Edmunds, Suffolk, IP33 3YB, UK.

Music Sales Pty Limited
20 Resolution Drive, Caringbah,
NSW 2229, Australia.

Order No. AM954877
ISBN 0-7119-7473-X
This book © Copyright 1999 Wise Publications,
a division of Music Sales Limited.

Unauthorised reproduction of any part of this
publication by any means including photocopying is
an infringement of copyright.

Compiled by Jack Long.
New music engravings by
Enigma Music Production Services.
Cover design by Studio Twenty, London.

Printed in the EU.

Your Guarantee of Quality:
As publishers, we strive to produce every book to
the highest commercial standards.
This book has been carefully designed to minimise
awkward page turns and to make playing from it a real
pleasure. Particular care has been given to specifying
acid-free, neutral-sized paper made from pulps which
have not been elemental chlorine bleached. This pulp
is from farmed sustainable forests and was produced
with special regard for the environment.
Throughout, the printing and binding have been
planned to ensure a sturdy, attractive publication
which should give years of enjoyment.
If your copy fails to meet our high standards,
please inform us and we will gladly replace it.

Black Coffee *4*
Careless Whisper *6*
Harlem Nocturne *8*
How Insensitive *19*
I Won't Last A Day Without You *10*
Lily Was Here *12*
Lover Man (Oh Where Can You Be) *18*
Make It Easy On Yourself *20*
A Man And A Woman
(Un Homme Et Une Femme) *22*
Moonglow *25*
Move Closer *26*
The Nearness Of You *30*
Nights In White Satin *28*
Quiet Nights Of Quiet Stars (Corcovado) *48*
Solitude *32*
Songbird *34*
Stella By Starlight *31*
Stranger In Paradise *38*
Take My Breath Away *40*
Tonight *42*
Too Close For Comfort *44*
We've Only Just Begun *46*

Black Coffee

Words & Music by Paul Francis Webster & Sonny Burke

© Copyright 1948, 1949 & 1954 Webster Music Company & Sondot Music Corporation, USA.
Chelsea Music Publishing Company Limited, 124 Great Portland Street, London W1 (50%)/
BMG Music Publishing Limited, Bedford House, 69-79 Fulham High Street, London SW6 (50%).
This arrangement © Copyright 1999 BMG Music Publishing Limited for their share of interest.
All Rights Reserved. International Copyright Secured.

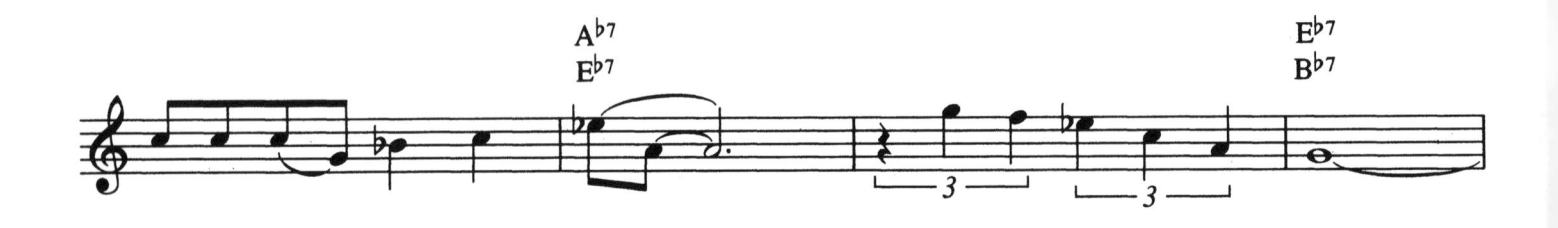

A♭m E♭m
E♭m B♭m
A♭m E♭m
Fm7(♭5) Cm7(♭5)
B♭7(♯9) F7(♯9)
E♭ B♭
F♯m7 D♭m7
B7 G♭7
E C♭
F♯m7 D♭m7
B7 G♭7
Fm7 Cm7
B♭7 F7
E♭7 B♭7
A♭7 E♭7
E♭7 B♭7
C7 G7
Fm7 Cm7
B♭7 F7
E♭ B♭

Careless Whisper

Words & Music by George Michael & Andrew Ridgeley

© Copyright 1984 Morrison Leahy Music Limited, 1 Star Street, London W2.
All Rights Reserved. International Copyright Secured.

Gm Dm
Dm Am
Am Em
Dm Am
Gm Dm
Dm Am
Am Em
1.
Dm Am
Gm Dm
Dm Am
Am Em
Dm Am
Gm Dm
Dm Am
Am Em
Dm Am
Gm Dm
Dm Am
Am Em
Dm Am
Am Em
2.
D.S. al Coda
CODA
A E
A7 E7
Dm Am

Harlem Nocturne

Music by Earle Hagen
Words by Dick Rogers

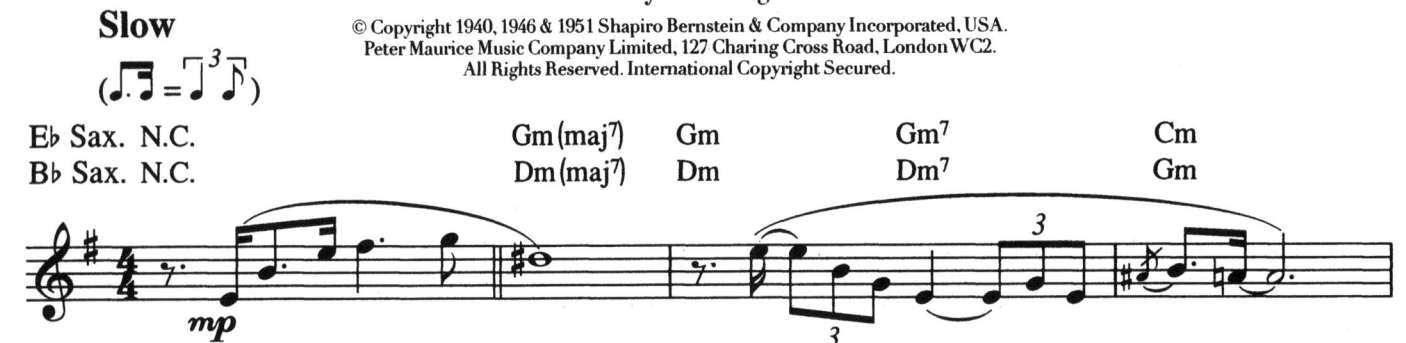

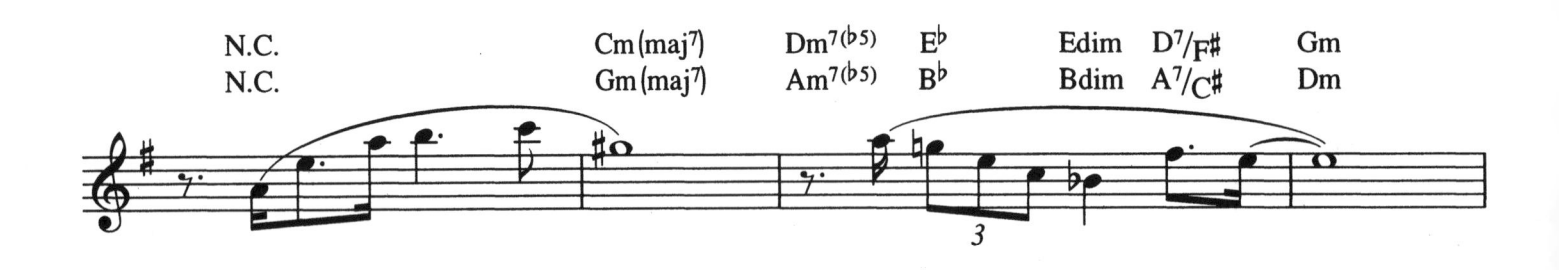

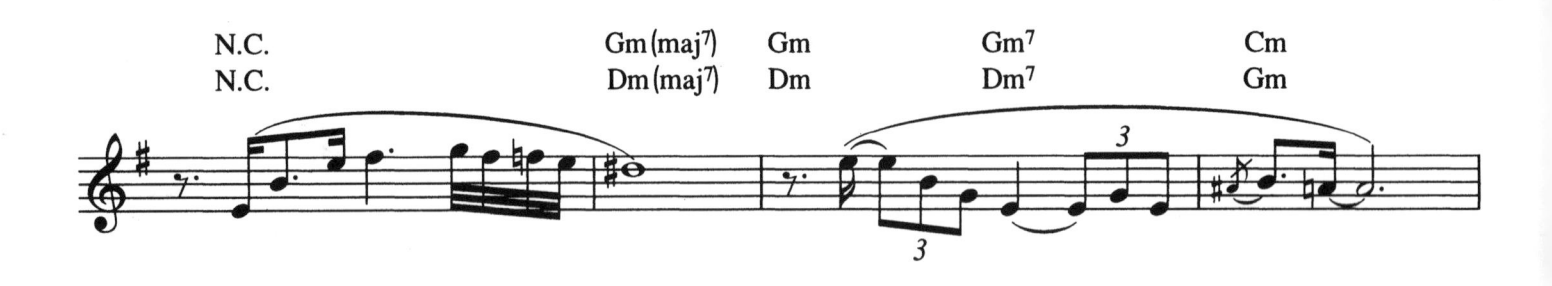

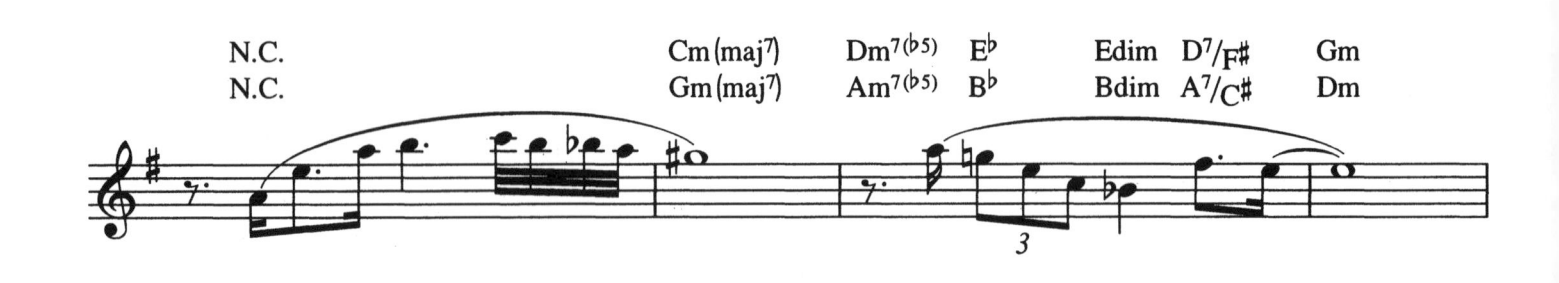

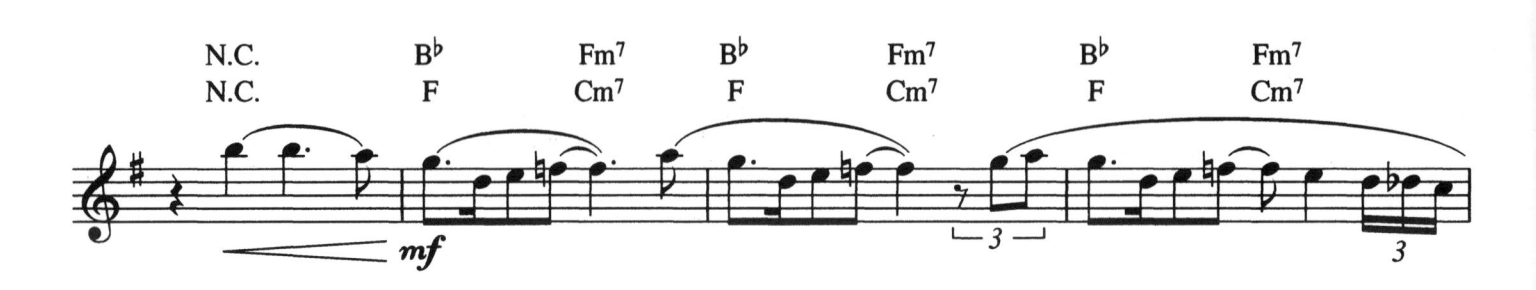

© Copyright 1940, 1946 & 1951 Shapiro Bernstein & Company Incorporated, USA.
Peter Maurice Music Company Limited, 127 Charing Cross Road, London WC2.
All Rights Reserved. International Copyright Secured.

B♭ F
B♭7 F7
E♭ B♭
B♭m7 Fm7
E♭ B♭
B♭m7 Fm7
Gm7(♭5) Dm7(♭5)
G♭9 (No 3rd) D♭9 (No 3rd)
F7 C7
B♭ F
Fm7 Cm7
B♭ F
Fm7 Cm7
B♭ F
Fm7 Cm7
mf
B♭ F
B♭7 F7
E♭ B♭
B♭m7 Fm7
E♭ B♭
B♭m7 Fm7
Gm7(♭5) Dm7(♭5)
G♭9 (No 3rd) D♭9 (No 3rd)
F7 C7
D7(♯9) A7(♯9)
Gm add9 Dm add9
N.C. N.C.
Gm (maj7) Dm (maj7)
mp
Gm Dm
Gm7 Dm7
Cm Gm
N.C. N.C.
Cm (maj7) Gm (maj7)
Dm7(♭5) Am7(♭5)
E♭ B♭
Edim Bdim
D7/F♯ A7/C♯
Gm Dm
Cm7 Gm7
Cm6 Gm6
Gm Dm

I Won't Last A Day Without You

Words by Paul Williams
Music by Roger Nichols

© Copyright 1971 Almo Music Corporation, USA.
All rights for the British Commonwealth (excluding Canada & Australasia)
controlled by Rondor Music (London) Limited, 10a Parsons Green, London SW6.
All Rights Reserved. International Copyright Secured.

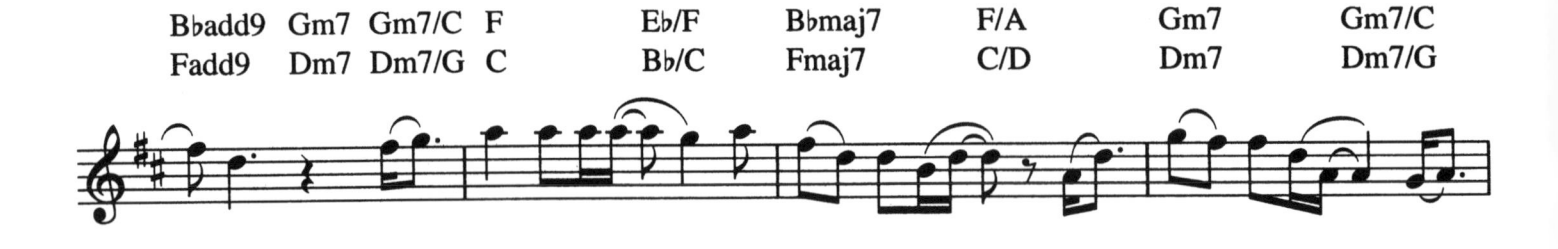

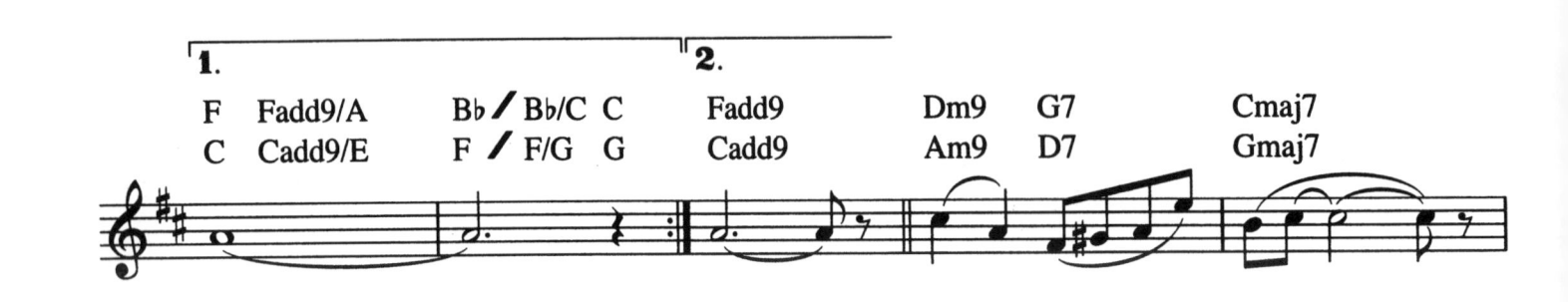

Dm7 G7 Asus4 A Bm7 E7 A
Am7 D7 Esus4 E F♯m7 B7 E
F♯m7 G Asus4 A Gm7 C7 F Am7
C♯m7 D Esus4 E Dm7 G7 C Em7
B♭ B♭/C Dm9 Gm7 Gm7/C F Am7
F F/G Am9 Dm7 Dm7/G C Em7
B♭ B♭/C Dm9 Gm7 Gm7/C F E♭/F
F F/G Am9 Dm7 Dm7/G C B♭/C
B♭add9 Gm7 Gm7/C F E♭/F B♭add9 Gm7 Gm7/C F E♭/F
Fadd9 Dm7 Dm7/G C B♭/C Fadd9 Dm7 Dm7/G C B♭/C
B♭maj7 F/A 1. Gm7 Gm7/C Fadd9/C Gm7/C
Fmaj7 C/E Dm7 Dm7/G Cadd9/G Dm7/G
2. Gm7 C7sus4 F Fadd9/A B♭add9 / B♭add9/C C Fadd9
Dm7 G7sus4 C Cadd9/E Fadd9 / Fadd9/G G Cadd9

Lily Was Here

Music by David A. Stewart

© Copyright 1989 D'N'A Limited/BMG Music Publishing Limited,
All rights administered by BMG Music Publishing Limited, Bedford House, 69-79 Fulham High Street, London SW6 3JW.
This arrangement © Copyright 1999 BMG Music Publishing Limited.
All Rights Reserved. International Copyright Secured.

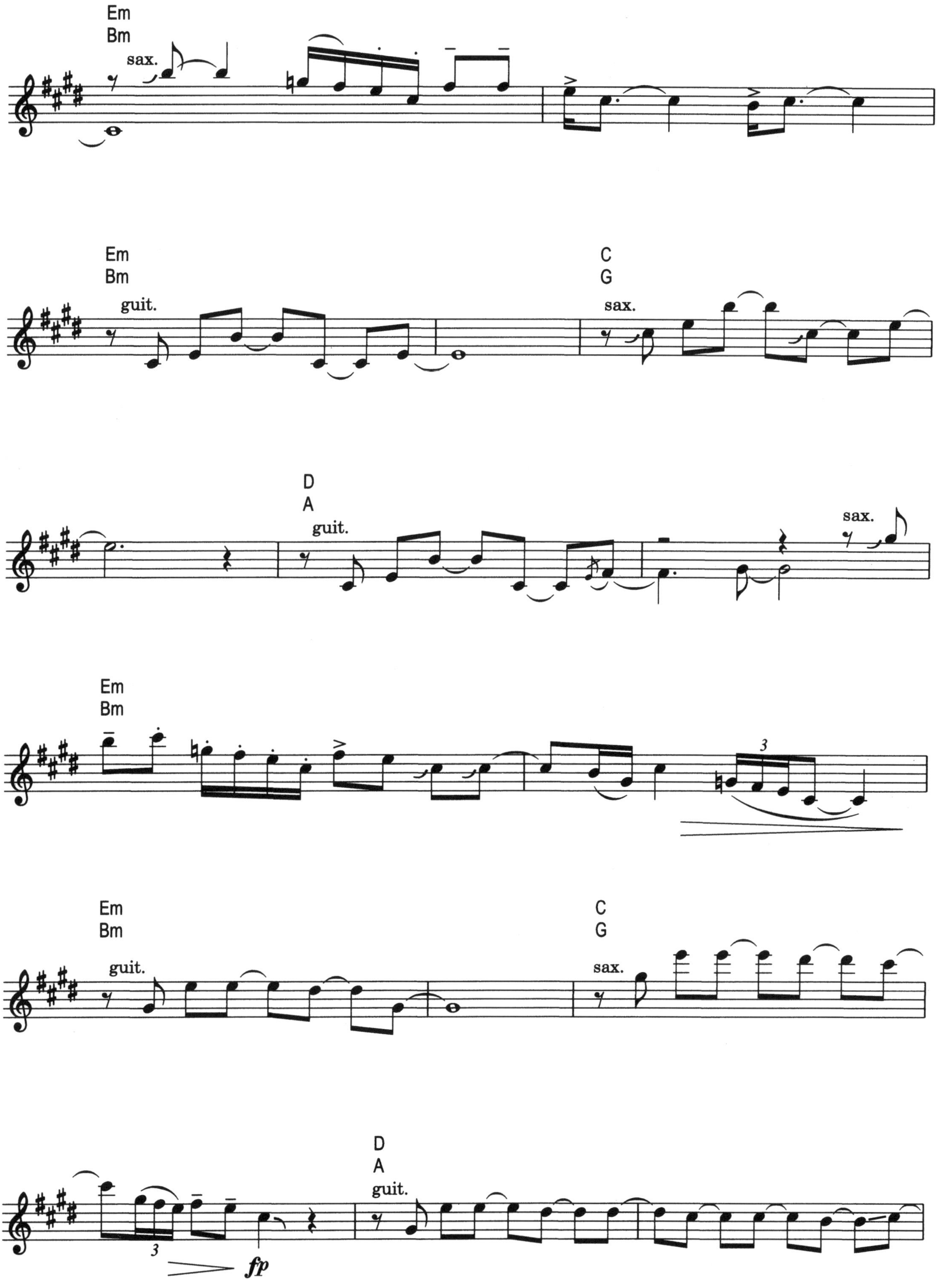
Em
Bm
sax.
guit.
C
G
D
A
3
fp

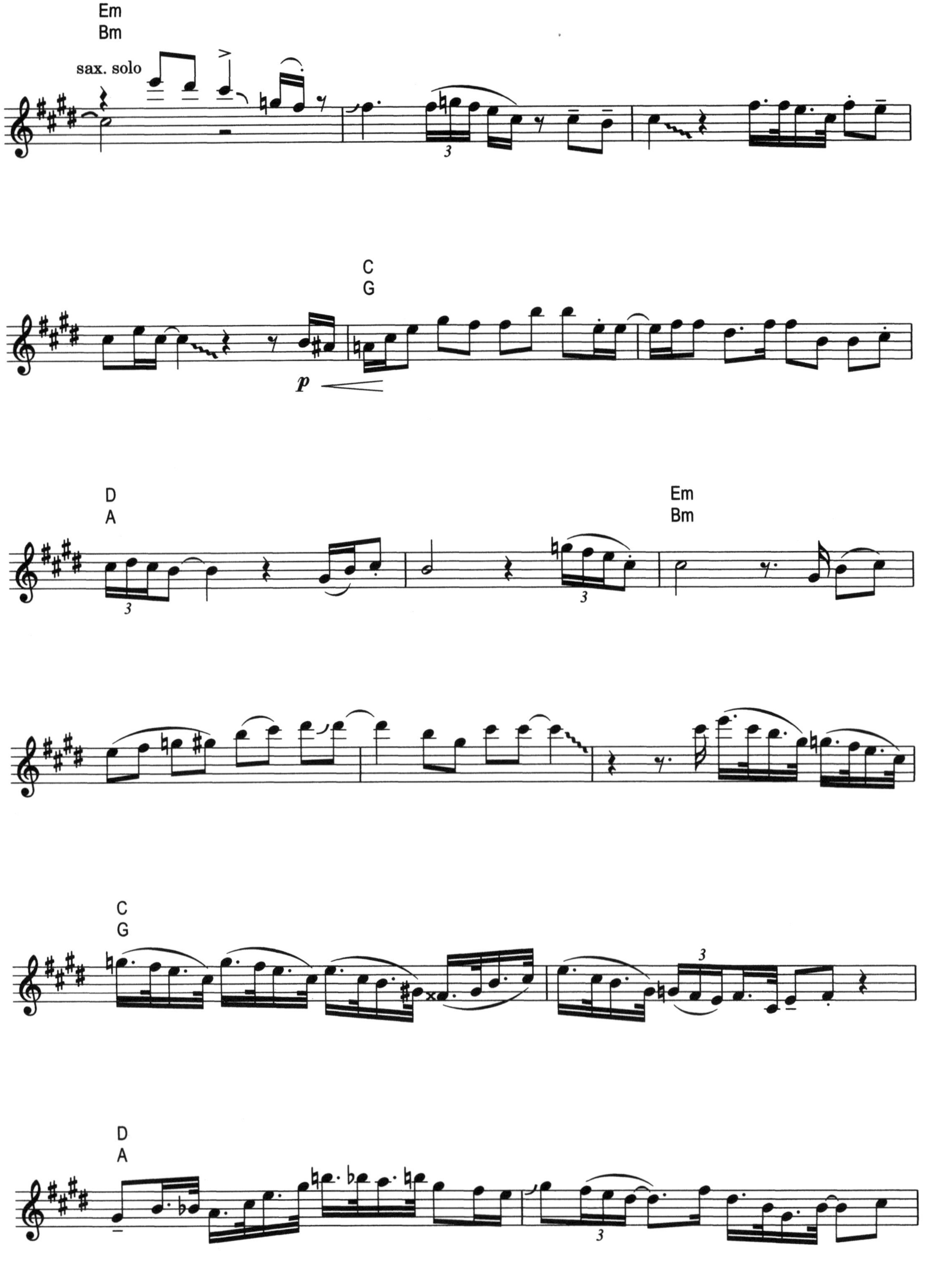
Em
Bm
sax. solo
C
G
p
D
A
Em
Bm
C
G
D
A

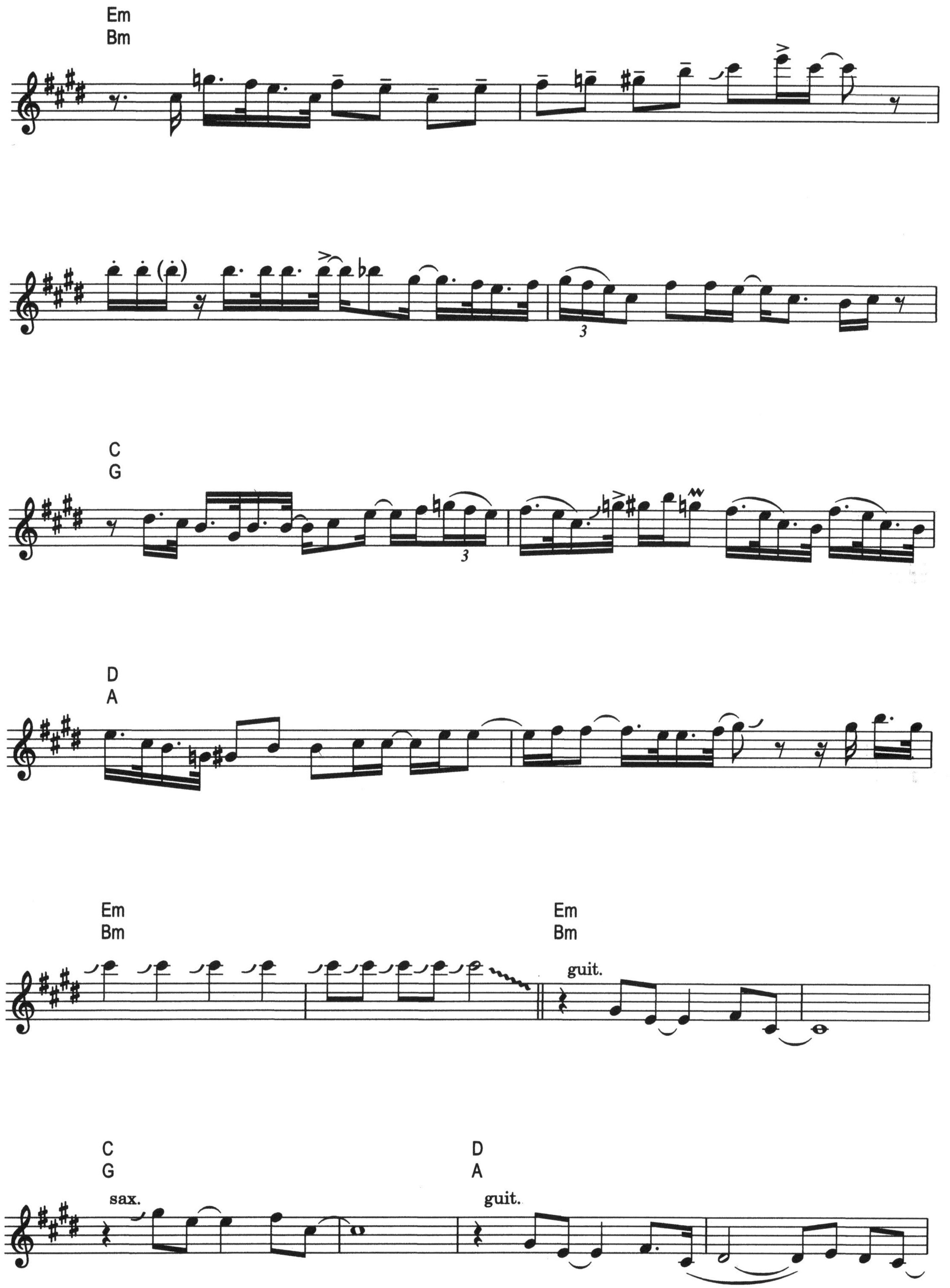
Em
Bm
C
G
D
A
Em
Bm
Em
Bm
guit.
C
G
sax.
D
A
guit.

Em
Bm
sax.
Em
Bm
guit.
sax.
C
G
D
A
guit.
sax.
Em
Bm
guit.
C
G
sax.
D
A
guit.
Em
Bm
sax.
guit.
sax.
C
G
D
A
guit.

Em
Bm
sax.
C
G
sax.
guit.
D
A
sax.
guit.
guit.
Em
Bm
sax.
guit.
C
G
guit.
sax.
guit.
D
A
sax.
Em
Bm
Em
Bm

Lover Man (Oh Where Can You Be)

Words & Music by Jimmy Davis, Roger Ram Ramirez & Jimmy Sherman

© Copyright 1944 MCA Music (a division of MCA Incorporated, USA).
MCA Music Limited, 77 Fulham Palace Road, London W6 for the World
(excluding North, South and Central America, Japan, Australasia and the Philippines).
All Rights Reserved. International Copyright Secured.

How Insensitive

Music by Antonio Carlos Jobim. Original Lyrics by Vinicius De Moraes.
English Lyrics by Norman Gimbel

© Copyright 1963, 1964 by Antonio Carlos Jobim and Vinicius De Moraes, Brazil.
MCA Music Limited, 77 Fulham Palace Road, London W6 for the British Commonwealth (excluding Canada),
South Africa, Continent of Europe (excluding Italy, France, its Colonies, Protectorates and
Mandated Territories, Algeria, Tunisia, Morocco, Andorra and Monaco).
All Rights Reserved. International Copyright Secured.

Make It Easy On Yourself

Music by Burt Bacharach
Words by Hal David

© Copyright 1962 New Hidden Valley Music Company & Casa David Music Incorporated, USA.
MCA Music Limited, 77 Fulham Palace Road, London W6 (50%)/
Windswept Pacific Music Limited, Hope House, 40 St. Peter's Road, London W6 (50%).
All Rights Reserved. International Copyright Secured.

C7 C13 C7 Am7 Dm7 Bbmaj7 C13 C7 Am7 Dm7
G7 G13 G7 Em7 Am7 Fmaj7 G13 G7 Em7 Am7
Bbmaj7 C13 C7 Bbmaj9 C7sus4 C7 Fmaj7
Fmaj7 G13 G7 Fmaj9 G7sus4 G7 Cmaj7
3
C13 C7 Am7 Dm7 Bbmaj7 C13 C7 Am7 Dm7
G13 G7 Em7 Am7 Fmaj7 G13 G7 Em7 Am7
Bbmaj7 C13 C7 Bbmaj9 C7sus4 C7 Fmaj7
Fmaj7 G13 G7 Fmaj9 G7sus4 G7 Cmaj7
Am Bb C6 Fmaj7
Em F G6 Cmaj7
C13 C7 Am7 Dm7 Bbmaj7 C13 C7
G13 G7 Em7 Am7 Fmaj7 G13 G7
rit.
Am7 Dm7 Bbmaj7 C13 C7 Bbmaj9
Em7 Am7 Fmaj7 G13 G7 Fmaj9
a tempo
rit.
C7sus4 C7 F Bb6/F F
G7sus4 G7 C F6/C C

A Man And A Woman
(Un Homme Et Une Femme)

Original Words by Pierre Barouh. English Lyric by Jerry Keller. Music by Francis Lai

© Copyright 1966 Editions Saravah, France.
MCA Music Limited, 77 Fulham Palace Road, London W6 for the British Commonwealth, Eire, South Africa & the USA.
All Rights Reserved. International Copyright Secured.

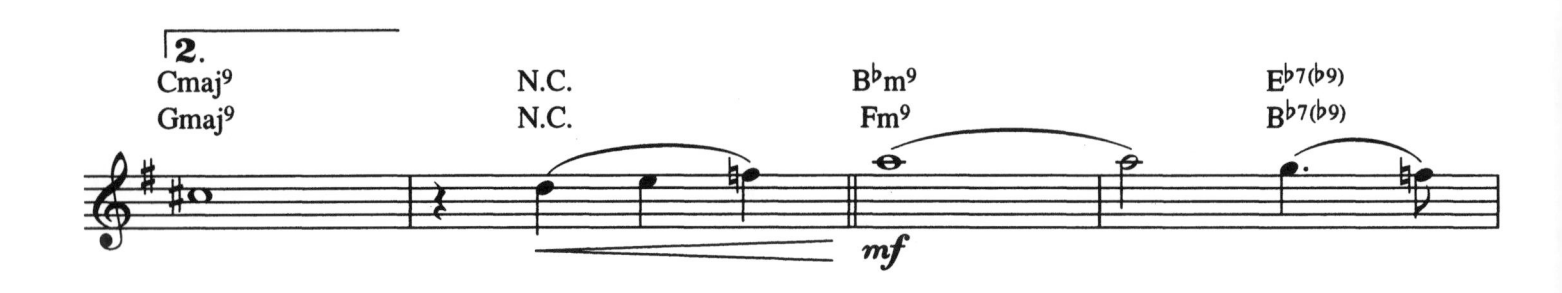

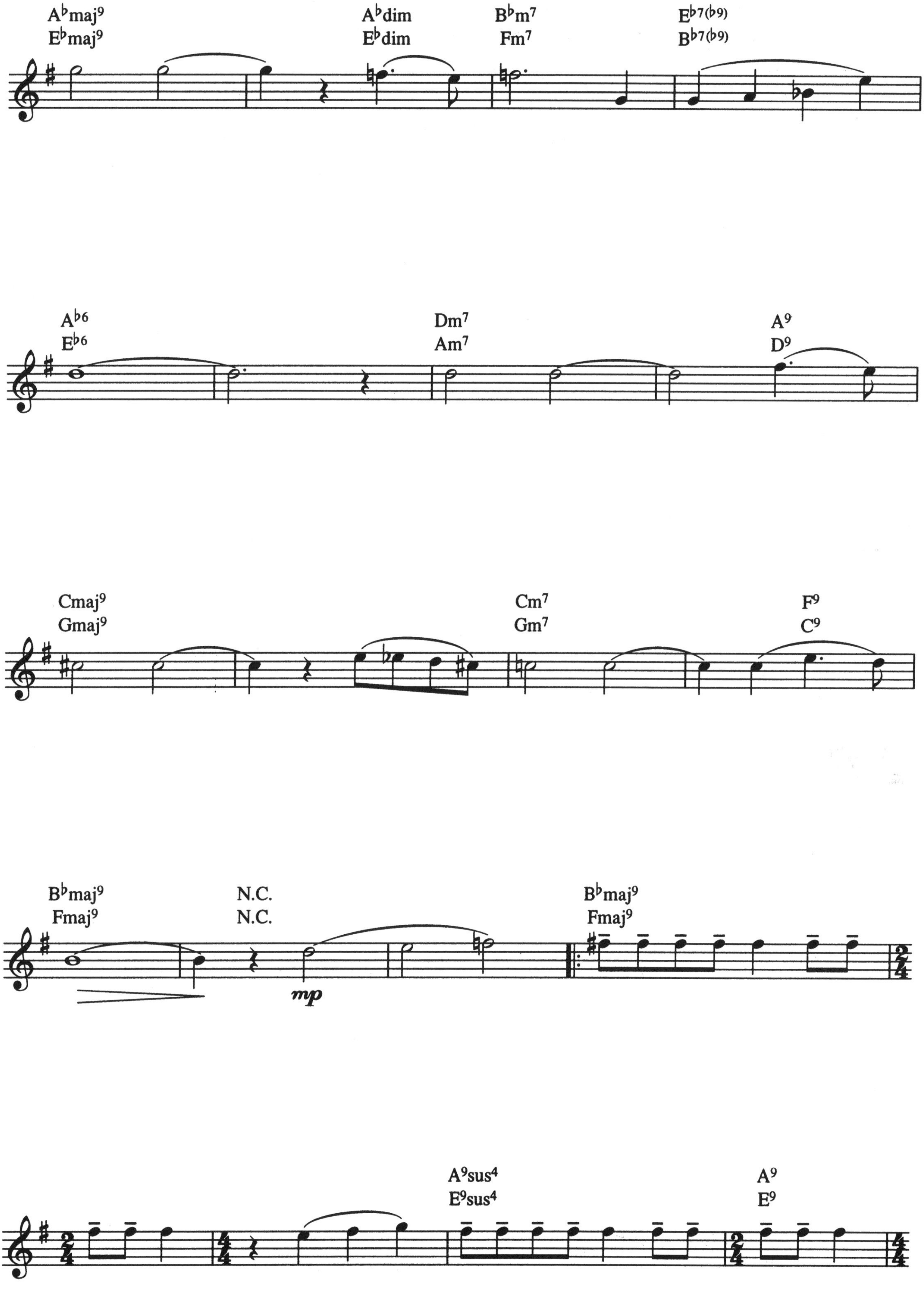
A♭maj9
E♭maj9
A♭dim
E♭dim
B♭m7
Fm7
E♭7(♭9)
B♭7(♭9)
A♭6
E♭6
Dm7
Am7
A9
D9
Cmaj9
Gmaj9
Cm7
Gm7
F9
C9
B♭maj9
Fmaj9
N.C.
N.C.
mp
B♭maj9
Fmaj9
A9sus4
E9sus4
A9
E9

A♭maj9
E♭maj9
G9sus4
D9sus4
G7(♭9)
D7(♭9)
1.
Cmaj9
Gmaj9
N.C.
N.C.
2.
Cmaj9
Gmaj9
Dm7
Am7
G9
D9
Cmaj9
Gmaj9
Dm7
Am7
G11
D11
Cmaj9
Gmaj9
mf
C♭maj9
G♭maj9
B♭maj9
Fmaj9
1.
2.
poco rit.
C♭maj9
G♭maj9
C♭maj9
G♭maj9
Cmaj9
Gmaj9
mp
pp

Moonglow

Words & Music by Will Hudson, Eddie de Lange & Irving Mills

© Copyright 1934 Exclusive Publications Incorporated, USA. Copyright assigned 1934 to Mills Music Incorporated, USA.
Authorised for sale in the UK and Eire only by permission of Boosey & Hawkes Music Publishers Limited, London.
All Rights Reserved. International Copyright Secured.

Move Closer

Words & Music by Phyllis Nelson

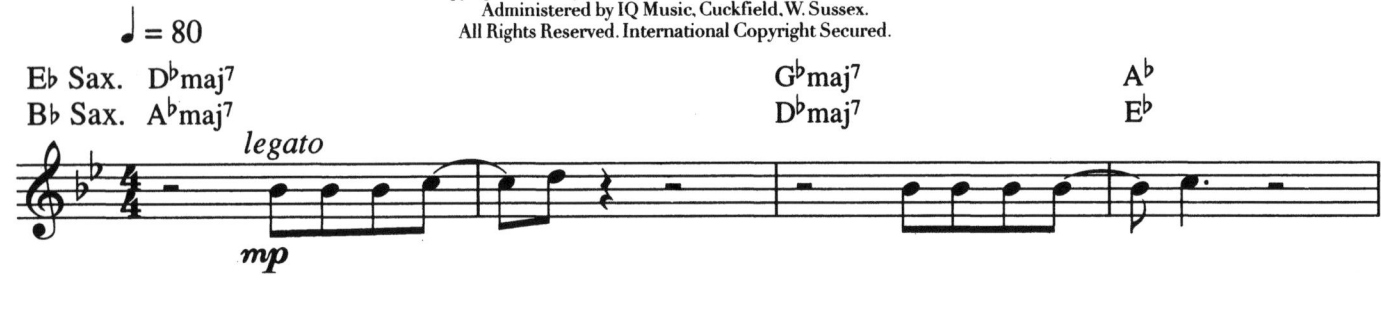

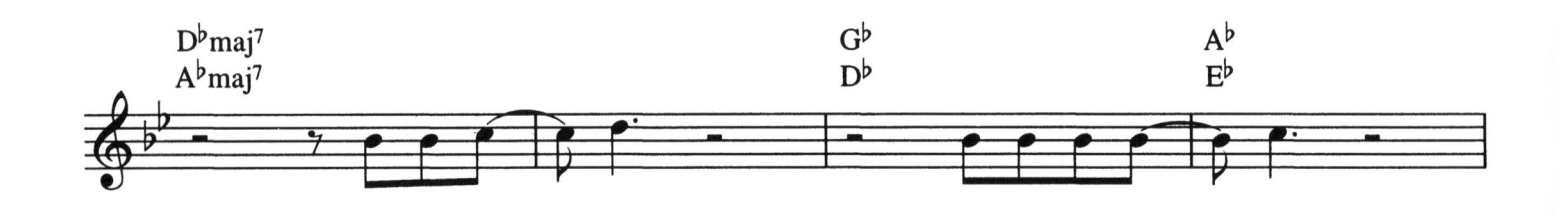

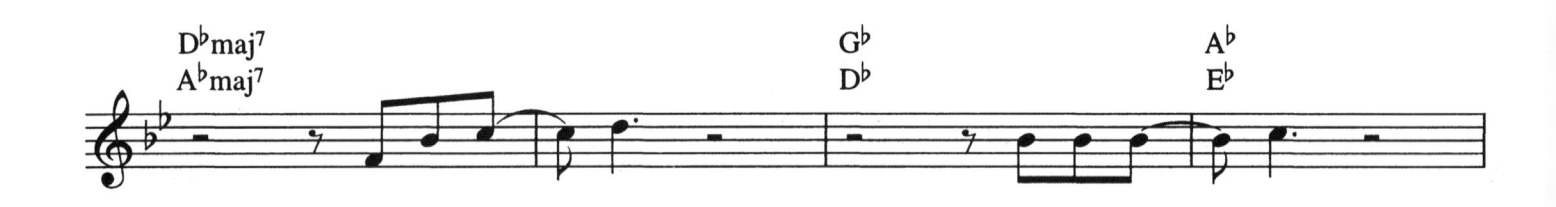

© Copyright 1985 Phyllis Nelson Music/American Summers Music.
Administered by IQ Music, Cuckfield, W. Sussex.
All Rights Reserved. International Copyright Secured.

G♭ D♭
A♭ E♭
G♭maj7 D♭maj7
To Coda
D♭maj7 A♭maj7
G♭maj7 D♭maj7
A♭ E♭
D♭maj7 A♭maj7
G♭maj7 D♭maj7
A♭ E♭
D♭maj7 A♭maj7
G♭ D♭
A♭ E♭
D♭maj7 A♭maj7
G♭ D♭
A♭ E♭
D.S. al Coda
CODA
D♭maj7 A♭maj7
G♭maj7 D♭maj7
A♭ E♭
Repeat to fade

Nights In White Satin

Words & Music by Justin Hayward

© Copyright 1967 by Tyler Music Limited, Suite 2.07, Plaza 535 Kings Road, London SW10.
All Rights Reserved. International Copyright Secured.

Dm Am
C G
Dm Am
C G
mp
B♭ F
A E
Dm Am
C G
B♭ F
A E
Dm Am
B♭ F
Dm Am
B♭ F
Gm Dm
A E
Gm Dm
A E
D.C. al Coda
Dm Am
C G
B♭ F
Dm Am
C G
Dm Am
C G
gliss.
mf
CODA
B♭ F
Dm Am
C G
Dm Am
C G
Dm Am
G D
B♭ F
Dm Am
C G
Dm Am
C G
Dm Am

The Nearness Of You

Music by Hoagy Carmichael
Words by Ned Washington

© Copyright 1937, 1940 renewed 1964, 1967 Famous Music Corporation, USA.
All Rights Reserved. International Copyright Secured.

Stella By Starlight

Music by Victor Young
Words by Ned Washington

© Copyright 1944 Famous Music Corporation, USA.
All Rights Reserved. International Copyright Secured.

Medium slow

Solitude

Words by Eddie de Lange & Irving Mills
Music by Duke Ellington

© Copyright 1934 Milsons Music Publishing Corporation, USA.
Sole agents for British Empire (excluding Canada) and Europe J. R. Lafleur & Son Limited.
Authorised for sale in the UK by Permission of Boosey & Hawkes Music Publishers Limited, London.
All Rights Reserved. International Copyright Secured.

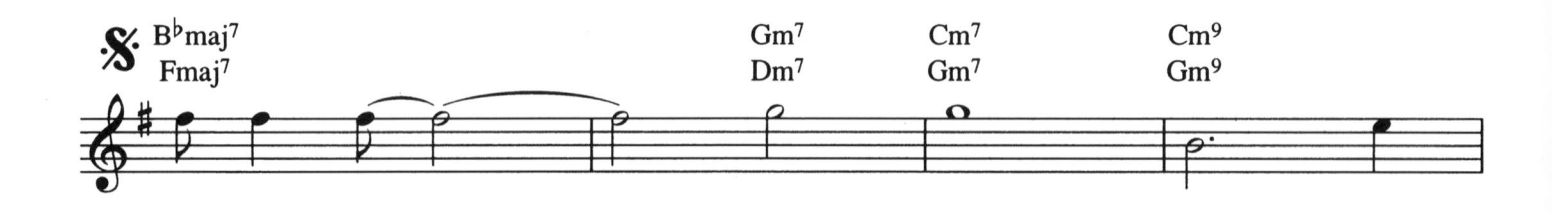

E♭6 Cm7 C♯dim B♭/D B♭6 B♭dim F9 F7aug
B♭6 Gm7 G♯dim F/A F6 Fdim C9 C7aug
B♭maj7 Gm7 Cm7 Cm9
Fmaj7 Dm7 Gm7 Gm9
D.𝄋 al Coda
E♭/F Dm/F Cm7/F F7(♭9) B♭maj7 Cm9 F7aug
B♭/C Am/C Gm7/C C7(♭9) Fmaj7 Gm9 C7aug
CODA
molto rit.
Cm7/F N.C. B♭ E♭9 B♭
Gm7/C N.C. F B♭9 F

Songbird

By Kenny G

© Copyright 1987 EMI Blackwood Music Incorporated, Kuzu Music, Brenee Music & High Tech Music, USA.
EMI Songs Limited, 127 Charing Cross Road, London W1.
All Rights Reserved. International Copyright Secured.

Bb7
F7
Ebm7
Bbm7
Dbmaj7
Abmaj7
Ebm7
Bbm7
Dbmaj7
Abmaj7
Ebm7
Bbm7
Dbmaj7
Abmaj7
Ebm7
Bbm7
Dbmaj7
Abmaj7
Ebm7
Bbm7
Fm7
Cm7
Gbmaj7
Dbmaj7
Fm7
Cm7
Ebm7
Bbm7
Fm7
Cm7
Bb7
F7
Bb7
F7
Ebm7
Bbm7
Bb7
F7

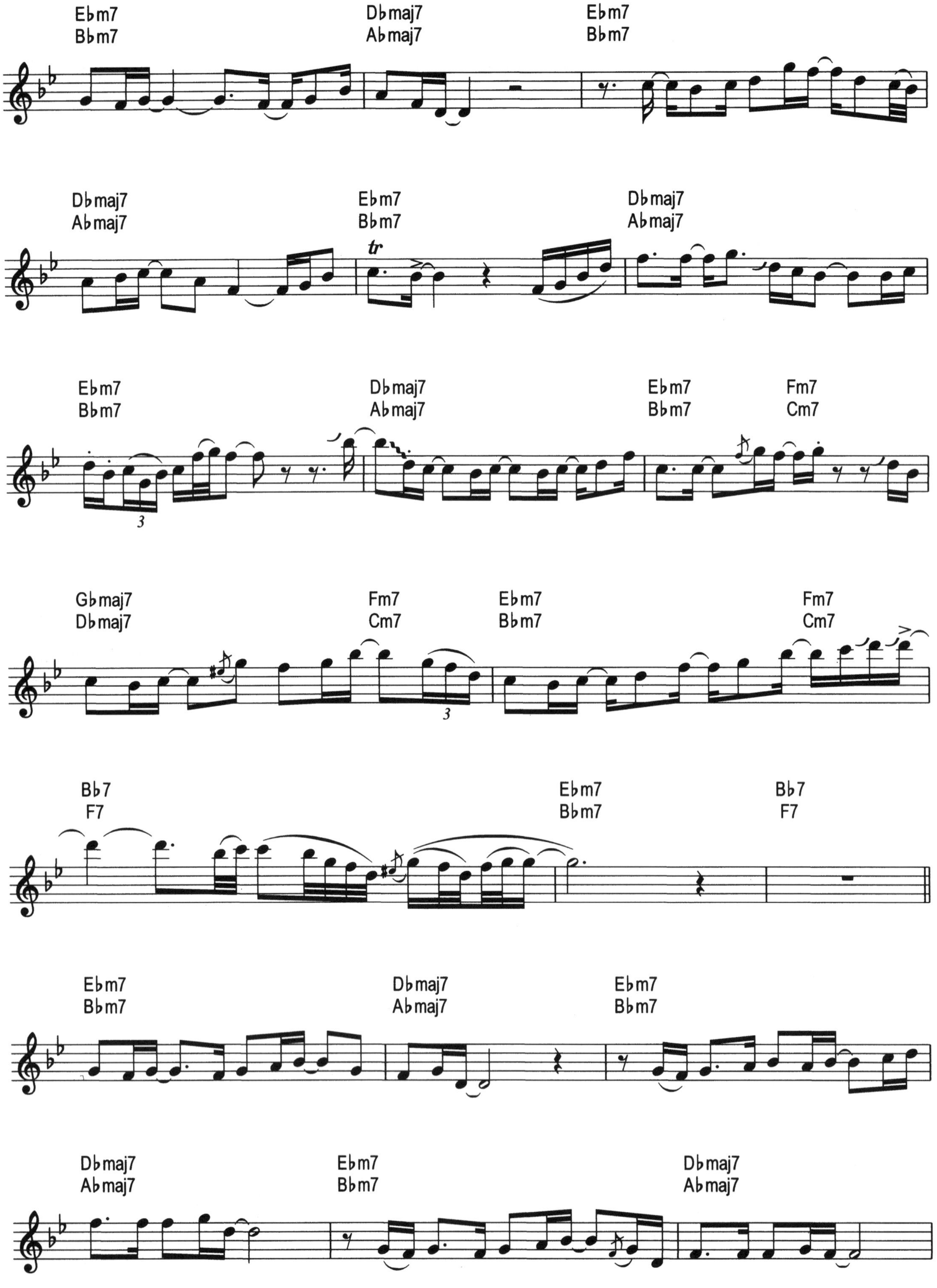

Ebm7
Bbm7
Dbmaj7
Abmaj7
Ebm7
Bbm7
Fm7
Cm7
Gbmaj7
Dbmaj7
Fm7
Cm7
Ebm7
Bbm7
Fm7
Cm7
Bb7
F7
Ebm7
Bbm7
Fm7
Cm7
Gbmaj7
Dbmaj7
Fm7
Cm7
Ebm7
Bbm7
Fm7
Cm7
Bb7
F7
Ebm7
Bbm7
Fm7
Cm7
Gbmaj7
Dbmaj7
Ebm7
Bbm7
Fm7
Cm7
Bb7
F7
Ebm7
Bbm7
Dbmaj7
Abmaj7

Stranger In Paradise

Words & Music by Robert Wright & George Forrest

© Copyright 1953 Scheffel Music Corporation, USA.
Warner Chappell Music Limited, Griffin House, 161 Hammersmith Road, London W6.
All Rights Reserved. International Copyright Secured.

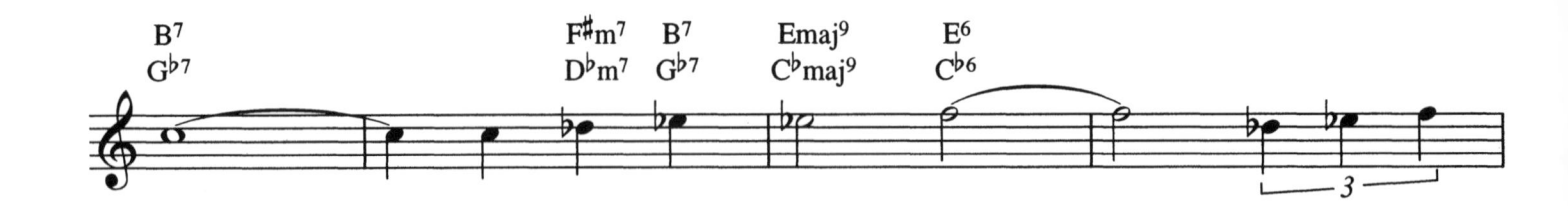

G7 Dm7 G7 Cmaj9 C6 Fm7
D7 Am7 D7 Gmaj7 G6 Cm7
B♭7 E♭maj7 C7(♭9) Fm7
F7 B♭maj7 G7(♭9) Cm7
B♭7 E♭maj7 E♭6 Fm7
F7 B♭maj7 B♭6 Cm7
A♭m6 B♭7 E♭6 Gm Cm7 F7
E♭m6 F7 B♭6 Dm Gm7 C7
3
B♭7 E♭maj7 Gm7(♭5) C7 C7(♭9) Fm7
F7 B♭maj7 Dm7(♭9) G7 G7(♭9) Cm7
1. 2.
A♭m6 B♭7 E♭ A♭m E♭ Edim E♭ A♭m E♭
E♭m6 F7 B♭ E♭m B♭ Bdim B♭ E♭m B♭

Take My Breath Away

Words by Tom Whitlock
Music by Giorgio Moroder

© Copyright 1986 Budde Music & Famous Music Corporation (25%), USA.
Warner Chappell Music Limited, Griffin House, 161 Hammersmith Road, London W6 (50%)/GEMA (25%).
All Rights Reserved. International Copyright Secured.

2.
E♭ B♭
Fm Cm
Cm/G Gm/D
A♭ E♭
B♭ F
E♭/G B♭/D
D♭ A♭
A♭ E♭
B♭ F
E♭/G B♭/D
D♭ A♭
A♭ E♭
B♭ F
E♭ B♭
A♭ E♭
Cm/G Gm/D
Fm Cm
1.
Cm/G Gm/D
2.
Cm/G Gm/D
D.C. al Coda
CODA
rit.
A♭ E♭
Cm/G Gm/D
Cm Gm
D♭ A♭
E♭ B♭
A♭ E♭

Tonight

Music by Leonard Bernstein
Lyrics by Stephen Sondheim

© Copyright 1956, 1957, 1958, 1959 by the Estate of Leonard Bernstein & Stephen Sondheim.
Copyright renewed. Leonard Bernstein Music Publishing Company LLC, Publisher. Boosey & Hawkes Incorporated, Sole agent.
Reproduced by permission of Boosey & Hawkes Music Publishers Limited, The Hyde, Edgware Road, London NW9.
All Rights Reserved. International Copyright Secured.

Beguine tempo

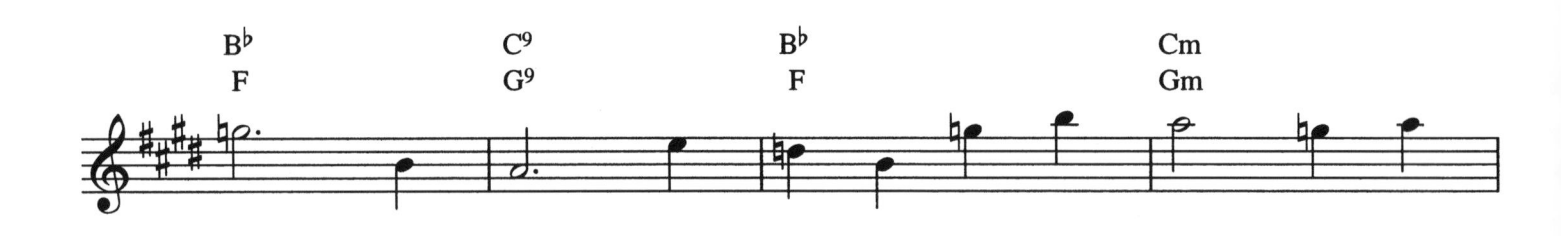

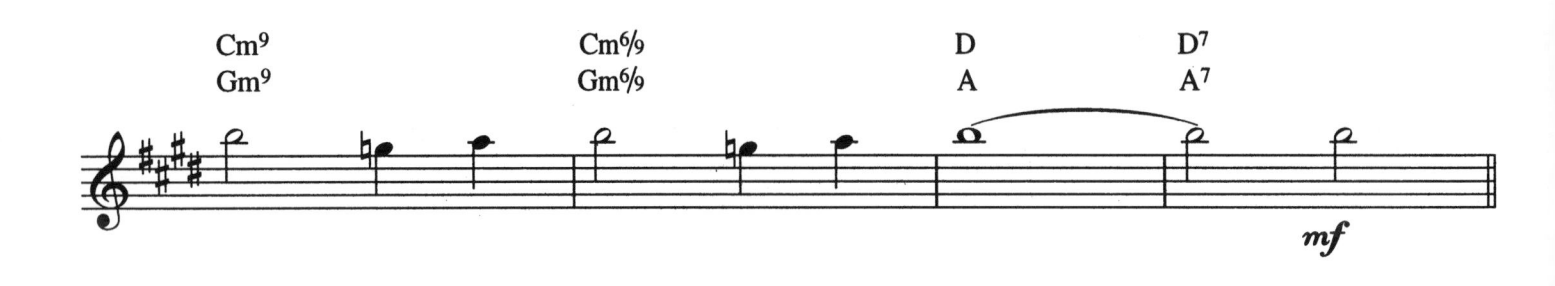

E♭ Cm6
B♭ Gm6
B♭m6 A7sus4 A7(♭5) D7
Fm6 E7sus4 E7(♭5) A7
mp
G A9 G Em7
D E9 D Bm7
1.
Bm Am7 D7(♭5) Gmaj7 Em7 Am7 D7
F♯m Em7 A7(♭5) Dmaj7 Bm7 Em7 A7
mf
2.
Gmaj7 Em7 Cmaj9 Gmaj9
Dmaj7 Bm7 Gmaj9 Dmaj9

Too Close For Comfort

Words & Music by Larry Holofcener, George Weiss & Jerry Bock

© Copyright 1957 Times Square Music Publications Company/Abilene Music Incorporated, USA.
Carlin Music Corporation, Iron Bridge House, 3 Bridge Approach, London NW1 (66.66%)/
Memory Lane Music Limited, 22 Denmark Street, London WC2 (33.33%).
All Rights Reserved. International Copyright Secured.

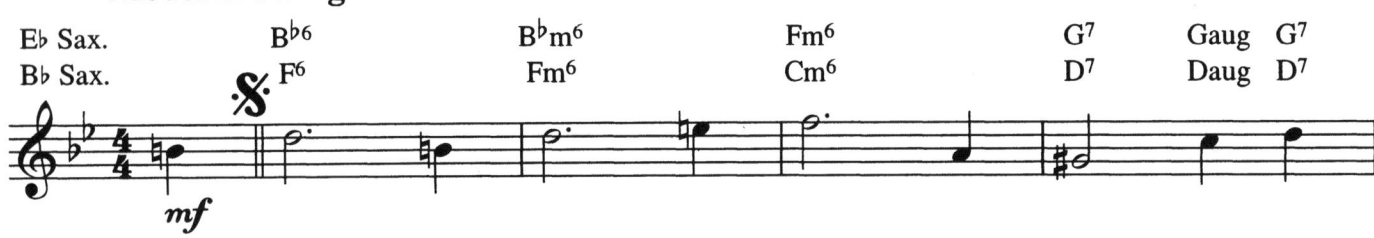

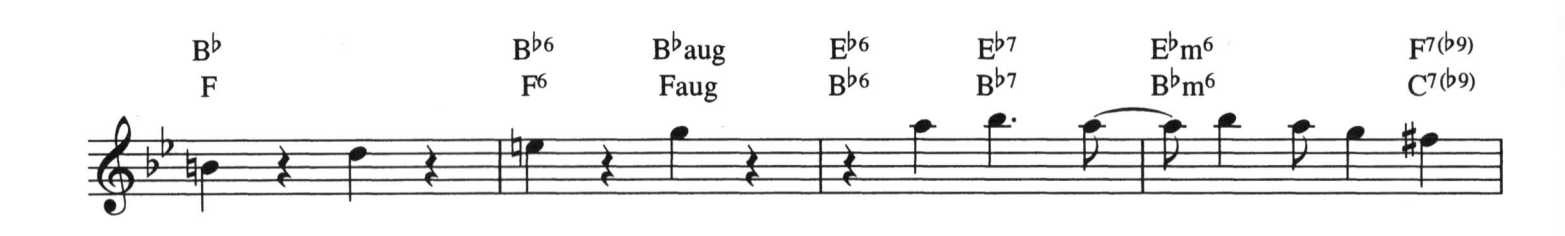

G♭7 F7 B♭6 B♭m6 Fm6
D♭7 C7 F6 Fm6 Cm6
G7 Gaug G7 E♭m6 F7 F7sus4 F7 B♭ B♭6 B♭aug
D7 Daug D7 B♭m6 C7 C7sus4 C7 F F6 Faug
E♭6 E♭7 E♭m6 F7(♭9) B♭m6 C7
B♭6 B♭7 B♭m6 C7(♭9) Fm6 G7
To Coda
D.S. al Coda
G♭9 F9 E♭m6 F7(♭9) B♭m C7 F7
D♭9 C9 B♭m6 C7(♭9) Fm G7 C7
CODA
B♭m B♭m7 B♭m6
Fm Fm7 Fm6
G♭9 F9 E♭m6 F7(♭9) B♭m
D♭9 C9 B♭m6 C7(♭9)) Fm

We've Only Just Begun

Words by Paul Williams
Music by Roger Nichols

© Copyright 1970 by Irving Music Incorporated, USA.
All rights for the British Commonwealth of Nations (excluding Canada and Australasia) and the
Republic of Eire controlled by Rondor Music (London) Limited, 10a Parsons Green, London SW6.
All Rights Reserved. International Copyright Secured.

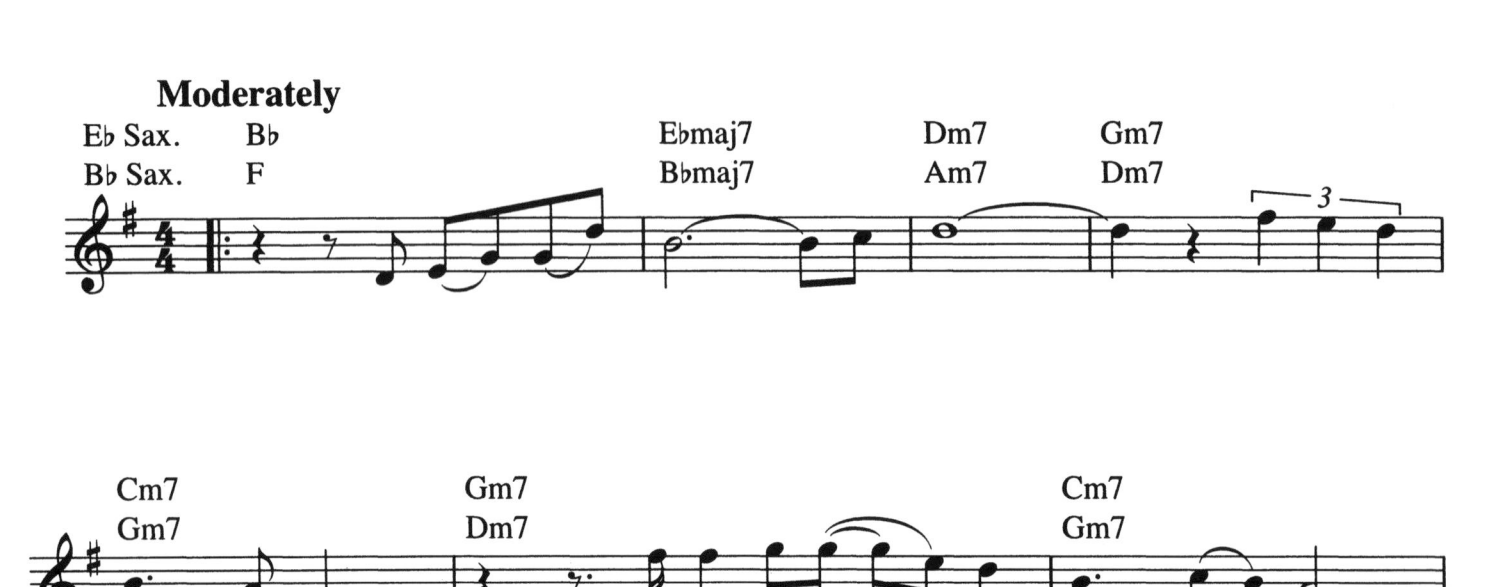

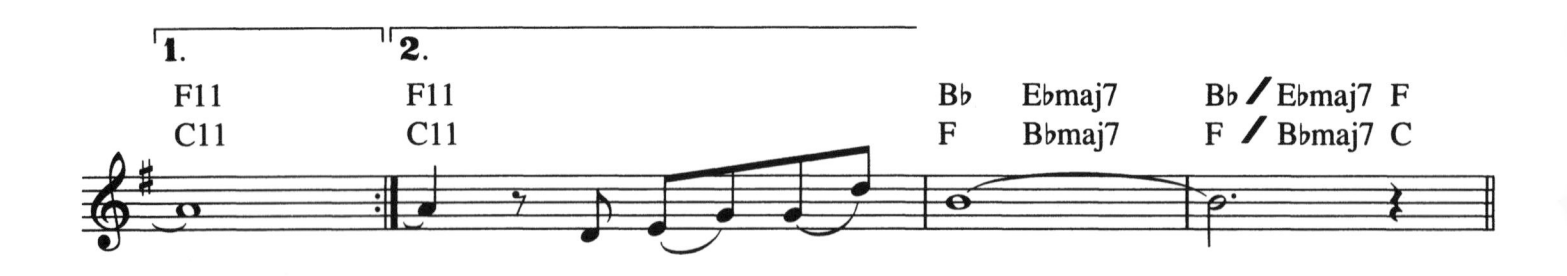

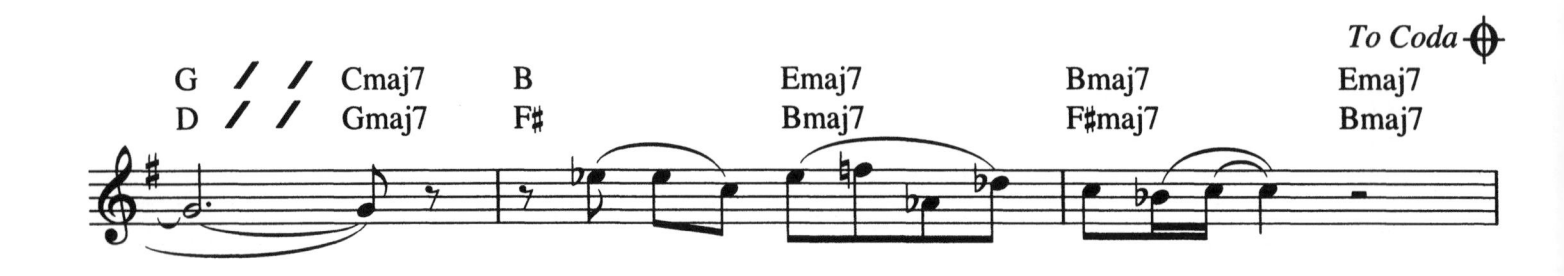

Moderately

Bmaj7
F♯maj7
Emaj7
Bmaj7
F11
C11
D.C. (2nd time only) al Coda
CODA
Bmaj7
F♯maj7
Emaj7
Bmaj7
F11
C11
B♭
F
E♭maj7
B♭maj7
Dm7
Am7
Gm7
Dm7
3
Cm7
Gm7
Gm7
Dm7
Cm7
Gm7
F11
C11
B♭maj7
Fmaj7
E♭maj7
B♭maj7
B♭maj7
Fmaj7
E♭maj7
B♭maj7
D
A

Quiet Nights Of Quiet Stars (Corcovado)

English Words by Gene Lees
Music & Original Words by Antonio Carlos Jobim

© Copyright 1962, 1965 by Antonio Carlos Jobim, Brazil.
MCA Music Limited, 77 Fulham Palace Road, London W6 for the
British Commonwealth (excluding Canada & South Africa).
All Rights Reserved. International Copyright Secured.

Bossa nova